The Cost of Daydreams

A poetry collection

By Melissa Bergsma

Contents

Black Dalia: foreboding

October's embrace 8
If I could bottle this place, I'd sell it for a smile 9
He's their age 11
Postmortem thickets 12
Time is never now, and abandon is rarely wild 13
I come with warning labels 14

Snapdragon: deception

Umbrella recommended 18
Death of Father Time 22
Full disclosure 26
I blame the weather 29

Lily of the Valley: pain

White noise 31
Toska 33
I uncork the self-loathing and pour out a few drops 35
Caustic distractions 36
The edge of sanity 37
But I don't want to hear my fortune 38
Shrinking 39
Unmade 40

Cyclamen: goodbye

Blood ink won't write you gone 42
Earth dies but we push on 44
The monsoon of his lament 47
Death comes but you can't remember if you said goodbye 48
Hookah bar nights 49
Moving forward 51

Nightshade: truth

My cloth cover 54
What's with trauma anyway 55
Mirage 57
Rise of the Autonomous 59
Beautifully wrapped fallacies 60
Buried treasure 61

Dandelion: rebirth

Pyromania is the least of my problems 63
Almost sunrise 64
Torrential acid...65
The changing tides..67
Hell must have a hell-of-a gym 69
Bloodied hands 71

Azalea: healing

Muddied shades of gray 73
Denouncing debilitating debris...75
Remembered identities..79
Memoirs of a caged bird 81

Iris: hope

Oil paint on a sharp tongue 85
Madness is a matter of perspective...87
When gas is $5/gallon but I can't breathe...91
Self-portrait...96

Magnolia: love of nature

Utterance in time 98
Tranquil mornings...101
The irony of warmth..102
Shrine to the red maple...103
Glazed over..106
Urban trance...107
Nature: my drug of choice 108

Monkey Face Orchid: humor & oddities

A good challenge is hard to resist..114
Well hello there..115
When the weather lets you down..117
Even the night sky is jealous..118
That little voice inside me needs reading material 119
Evensong..121
Fallen...123
Unearthing amnesia...125
Guardian archer 127
Power outages in my head 129
Infiltrated sleep..131
It's a coffee and f-bombs kind of day 132

Pink Camellia: longing

Empty afternoons 135
Auroras in Nod 137
The romans had it right 139
The mask I wear 141
Contused dawns between us 144
Ossature of daydreams 145

Ixora: passion

Caught in your trap 148
Ambrosia junkie 149
Broken timepiece 150
Confessions 151
Tangible sunrises 153
Unleashed 155
Leave nothing unscathed 157
Dysania 159
Untempered 161
Of electrified afternoons and toes that tingle 162
The inevitability of us 164

Honeysuckle: ceaseless love

The freefall 167
Embracing suspension 169
Integrated gravity 171
The architecture of us 173
Visceral 175
Exodus 177
I name you as my artist 179
Awake inside the gloaming 181
Transpose 183
Bleary and back 185
Anxiety's a cruel mistress 187
Wake me not 188
Pneumonic pigments 189
Weekdays without your wild 192
When there is beauty in being powerless 194

Glossary 197

About the author 200

For my rock, Nathan

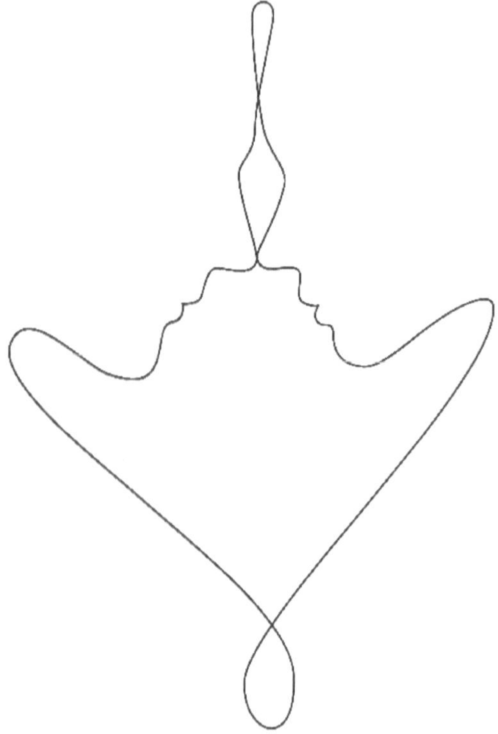

there are moments

    when I have the desperate need
    to immerse myself in poetry
    ingesting foreign syllables
    like midnight caffeine shots

a pull so vital
that denying it's power
would dredge a colony of honeybees
across over-sunned skin
caustically marring me
with delicate stingers

when nothing exists
apart from drowning
inside the ocean of
someone else's emotive punch

    moments

when sink or swim is relative
only to the writer

    but who am I
    when your words become me
    and my fingers
    are stained
    with your ink

Black Dalia

doom, or foreboding

October's Embrace

there was frost
     last night

like a dead omen
     left a bloody trail
         of white

            across the icy
              chapter

of this
once-warm
    expanse

If I could bottle this place, I'd sell it for a smile

an eerie silence
falls alongside frozen flakes
their magic consuming even the wind
I capture the quietude
stowing it away

these are easy the moments
the warmth of the sun in winter,
a meadowlark's melancholy song
crystalline powder being absorbed
into this frosted world

draped in seclusion's cloak
I could almost pretend
my ears don't strain for the
pressing *radditattat* of gunfire

I close my lids
and am overcome
by row upon row
of vacant strollers
with the brakes left on
carefully placed infant seats
cold from the same ice

that now cradles
their former wards

there are faint booms in the distance
the snow doing its best
to muffle the sobs of childless mothers
and all I can see
when my eyes open
is the red
of my umbrella

He's their age

I sent Tristan on his way
to the bus stop this morning
and read an email from the district
an hour later.
A kid brought bullets to school last week,
of course, they tell us today,
a week after the fact
now that more children are dead.

How do we move forward?
I refuse to allow anxiety and fear
to rule my days
but I can't keep them home forever.
Fuck this messed up world
where bullets talk
and children remain silent,
where the screams are muted
and anger festers beneath tears.

I'm parked in a field again,
Beacon sleeping at the wrong time
the way he always does
and nothing is beautiful.

Even the puffy clouds
just look like shadowed faces
screaming.

Postmortem Thickets

where does it go
when the cranes
have crooned their last
does time follow
when faltered
down a wayward path

elevated beyond the precipice
of mitigated wartime hues
where will we go
when the criers call out
in warning subterfuge

past postmortem thickets
will we find an end

drowning in our hatred
down this rugged, overgrown trail
in a mucked up lonely pond
seeking peace, to no avail

Time is never now &
abandon is rarely wild

he washed the night from my eyes in
a cascade of broken good mornings
and creamy gas station coffee
his lopsided grin making promises
that flushed my cheeks
and constricted the
empty cavity in my chest

but my tomorrow
was the shade of ancient lullabies
nearly forgotten shadows
that sought me out
to show me
where my cracks resided

like repaired porcelain
I tiptoed in an electric dance of
calculated risk
until my name
morphed to a whisper on his tongue
as days melded into weeks
and he mused over a shared future
like it didn't set his feet aflame

the driving urge to run doesn't chill
it burns

I come with warning labels

let not
the loosened tongue my pen wields,
spell you into her sultry tale

hold yourself at bay
ears shielded,
tucked secure inside your sacred
battle ground of least resistance

dirty fighting lies ahead,
no rules where echoes hide

she comes unbidden
as a geisha to your pith

master of a man's mind
syllables flow
synchronized in witty retort

I bottle her up
bury her in my darkest depths
but there are craters in the void
and cracks in the cork
she seems to seep through

I can't shake her,
this shadow,
that aches
for you to love me

her delicate fingers
strum lulling symphonies on
holographic piano keys
as she seeks to
enthrall your timeless spark

misguided talons spread wide my lips,
creeping out,
they grasp at lonely vessels

poison laced in your deepest desires
she tugs at strings you sought to keep tied

a talented masseuse
she caresses out kinks
from damaged arteries

not knowing how to fill them,
she abandons you to me

a wisp on the crisp inhale
this shadow has no beginning
that I might end her

step back,
don't fall for
this serene visage
a mirage of my fragmented psyche

I'll vanish
finding comfort in white noise
and empty bedroom walls

a disassociated spec of free

I'll warn you only once,
find your feet and

flee

Snapdragon

deception

Umbrella recommended

your constitution as fickle
as the coming storm

rolling in along once clear skies
like waves
stealing beneath the ocean's surface
breaking in startling crests
of alabaster mist
unleashing hordes of water
saved just for me

your words, forgotten symbols
etched in Sanskrit
on loose leaf canvases
I buried in caves
amidst the rumble
of your passing passions

like an unwanted sliver
wedged into the bed of my thumbnail
you bring about the recollection
of all those things
I once denied existence

yet here you remained
to my internal, utter irritation
scraping at floor boards

as they dragged you out

—

I woke mid storm last night
feeling insignificant
awed by the power

but I left the door closed
too afraid of standing in it
somehow knowing
you would strike me down

—

you left
like the morning after a storm
when the first rays of sunshine
begin to peek through remnants of
foreboding thunderheads as
they search out retreat

little puddles scattered
in patchwork spanning the driveway
splotches of dirty rain water
left in potholes

morning gives way to noon and
the sun evaporates

what remained of your moisture
and I can finally take a breath

I'm sure you blame me
likely saying
I was the catalyst to your demise,
that I was the weatherman
trapping you with my predictions

I know how much you loathe to be,
but
you're wrong

I am the hemlock tree
that weathered your wind and hail
in my strength, I bent
but never broke
and when you passed
I stood a little taller
having endured you

—

tiny ringlet clouds
now dot the sky
and I endeavor to stare at them
until they take form

this cobalt and ivory polka dot sky
is tinged with daunting gray and indigo
of your passing storm head

you'll recompose your pieces
unleash your illusory verbiage elsewhere

perhaps they will see you coming
taking cover
before you open your mouth

no one wants to dance with golf balls

Death of Father Time

perhaps the tomorrow you envision
differs from the gentle haze
of my yesterdays

maybe
yesterdays and tomorrows
are all illusory cosmic jokes
on our humanity

letting us believe that
time is relevant
all while the cosmos sits back
sipping sunsets
and getting drunk
on our delusional hypocrisies

we watch those same sunsets
mesmerized by their beauty
and find ourselves
finally unencrypted

those shackles
we were wearing
forged inside the labyrinth of
someone else's essence,
holographic projections
of the finest quality

pithy attempts at hindering us with numbers
enslaved in binding toil
until the monitors were turned off
for but a momentary lapse

the efforts of one
pivotal rebellious technician
who fought for us in secrecy

yes they exist as well
for evil cannot live
without the light to fight it
don't be obtuse
these are but scraps that segue
into the back alleys of our gameshow

—

the jackrabbits are flipping out
watching the magenta and pink
murk of dusk
dust these opaque movie screens
whispering its final farewells
as it searches out a lucid respite

tendrils of brume creeping over
once dangerous foliage,
patiently eating time

here I stand at the cusp of revelations
teetering at the end of time(s)

my wakened dreams
took a hammer
to the stopwatch
on my bedside table
and father time
is dying a slow
and painless death

hallucinations
can't feel pain, you see

the ever demanding paternity
streaming a litany of ticks at me
screaming nano seconds in
confused verbiage

I revel in the chaos
swimming in the knowing
that when the fog subsides
clarity reigns

still, day evolves to night
as it should
and as it will

morning hues
of the ever-rising sun
will greet us

they will not say
"how was your yesterday"

no,
they will infiltrate
your planted frame

singing
"welcome to today"

Full disclosure

I want to rip off that heart
that's sewn to my sleeve,
stomp on it,
and fuck you angry.

tear down hotel doors,
stare into your eyes and
use my hips, nails and teeth
to tell your body
how much you hurt me.
I want to mark you
like you have me...

then I want to be able to
walk away unscathed
to allow it to be over
before it ever really begins.

you pursued me,
when I was content alone,
made me vulnerable,
just to see if I could bleed.

you damaged me,
now, I'll always be searching for more...
for words that caress my skin.

I had no right to want you,
knowing we were doomed from hello.

I don't get attached to people,
it's not my way...
I don't do 'emotional'
I do 'cold'.

yet here I sit in my car biding
minutes as they sour to hours,
my cliché hope stretching
to its breaking point.

gray-blue clouds splotched as
sponge-work across an eerie peach skyline,
it moves with the wind,
like the tornado as it hits me

I warm my arms in
soothing horizontal motions
as I imagine a southern wind
carrying you home.

the concrete step in my barn
makes for a quiet respite
as I wait out the storm.
lightning strikes the ground
just yards from the door
and still, you haven't dialed my number,

what are the odds of that...
I know statistics,
I've checked accident reports like a fool,
looking for your name.

I keep turning my head at
the sound of tires on gravel,
or glancing up with each flash
on the road near my drive,
until I remember
you're not coming,
you never were.
a fading figment
of my optimist imagination.

I thought you were pressurized coal,
aged to perfection,
a priceless stone,
waiting for my artistry to carve you,
but you were just the pencil
shavings that slough off
when daylight stress revealed
your lies.

maybe I'm getting too old for adventure.

hell,
I don't even remember
what it tastes like.

I blame the weather

sandcastles,
constructed under a
piercing August gaze,
languidly deteriorate
inside the crushing typhoons
of mid-October
eroding into fragmented
crusty memories

caramel skin,
bleached ivory
by a waning winter sun

my complexion, a bleak
blinding thumbprint of
a lover's latent self-slaughter

Lily of the Valley

pain

White noise

I find myself caught
these weary evenings
in a ritual of poetry beyond dusk
blindly reading
while my other half sleeps

worry lurks at the fringes
a parasite that's embedded itself
one crimson scratch after another
infecting my every waking moment

widening my lids, I turn away
unshed water returning to the source
a practice I've slowly perfected
facade dropping only when darkness
embraces me in isolation
his torment need not my grief to add

I picture a life without him and
images come unbidden
like an old picture film
wreathed in silence,
my chest constricts
air frozen in collapsed lungs
as I fight for oxygen

I step across the threshold to
clammy skin and night sweats
where darkness swirls
and my helplessness
is a gut punch
keeping me dizzy

tortured by my
hopeless, useless self
shattered pieces of this lifeline
break off
and leave a trail of
sharp-edged bread crumbs
up to our quiet bedroom

skin cut open and bleeding
with each bare foot
that treads on his pain

I know the futility
in survivors guilt
when he's still here

so I wilt into this soft bed
and find myself praying
to any god that will listen

Toska

lounging in repose
surrounded by white-noise voices
whose tones rise and fall
with eager inflection

I listen without hearing
blankly staring at flurries
out the aged window pane
large, unwanted snowflakes
fighting one another
as they violently descend
from a slate gray skyline

guilt fills me as I embrace
the dull ache of being unfulfilled

a ping pushes rays
through thick cloud cover
but the warmth can't seem to stick
like a glimpse of spring in mid-May
it dissipates as soon as it arrives

leaving me in cooled blacks and whites
on this dreary afternoon
I step blindly,
pressing forward through
colorless minutes that drag

moments hit
that push me to the verge of tears
in-between the
d e a d   i n s i d e
extreme blocks of emotion
that I can't rightly name
entrap me in bouts of confusion
sitting here waiting for...
I don't know what

maybe that's why I feel vacant
having spent too many years
shoveling dirt over anything that hurts

not even sure what I'm looking for in this blizzard

I uncork the self-loathing and
pour out a few drops

   in artfully draped garnet lace
complete with
            bellybutton plunge and
just-above-the-ass dip

knocking back Grey Goose
on the rocks with lime

   selling myself
on cellophane lies
            and plastic smiles
   until nothing hurt

a defunct ticker
      doesn't shatter
when it hits the gravel at 160/mph

      it bounces

Caustic distractions

now and again
the fragments of
opaque wall-hangings
find retinue in
forgotten outcroppings

their dystopian speckles
a shelter from unspoken storms

the kind that char me
from the inside and
turn my tears to ash
before they surface

brazen
I counterstrike with a tender refrain
but like a dying fire, midwinter
upturned lips fail to warm

while my pupils see in metaphor
and every clock in the house
is prone to erratic outbursts

I rummage for scant moments
where I don't have to try
when my breath isn't laid heavy
by the oxygen my lungs rejected

The edge of sanity

a temporary object of lust
an image just as recyclable
as the bottle she drank dry
a body
a symbol
an idea, first beaten then let loose
a hand weakly grasping a blunt
a pair of lungs suffocated by the smoke
a girl enchanted by a promise
a mind blinded
a lie unraveled by reality
a single tear
a simple cut
a girl lost
a city Damned

I don't want to hear my fortune

beneath dank drapery
a withered oracle
whispered on a tepid draft

the lilting syllables
tumbling down morose axioms
to tend to my tired eardrums

she crooned of tragedy in the gutters
somewhere between the dead
and the disenfranchised

where the joker sat puffing his blunt and
pithily mocking our misfortune

saying they'll sing songs of our torment
with a dash of sarcasm
noting the irony of the rich
being so damn broken

plumes of smoke slowly curling skyward
there is no urgency to pain
it has nowhere better to be

Shrinking

it's a short drive home in the pitch
long before the winter sun wakes
to chase night into a corner

It's as if I go unnoticed
day by day
sinking a little deeper
into the tracts
my tears left behind
when I allowed them
to dry on my cheeks

I have forgotten
the viscosity of time
still, it grabs
me by the shoulders
to shake me awake
at the outer edge
of an unremembered cemetery

angry that I am no longer
the child who holds her breath in passing

I am the crack
in a moss-covered headstone
untended and overlooked

Unmade

she does not fear chaos
it's the wielding of silence
that haunts her

flickering in and out of permanence
as a sparkler foreseeing its end
her light, casually stolen
as quiet invades

merely a dying spark
discarded on the stained sidewalk
and left to fall into the space
where edges nearly touch

a chasm
brimming with unnoticed looks and
the purple bruises her teeth
left on her tongue

unassuming retort lands in the valleys
between vacant smiles
and hollow tears

so she dances alone
and in silence
she is unmade

Cyclamen

goodbye or resignation

Blood ink won't write you gone

i.

the clouded fingerlings
of my desire
fall from ashen skies
to rest on smothered
scraps of déjà vu

fanning out as
a panoramic kaleidoscope
for my viewing pleasure.

ii.

I don't want to watch you
through this lens
while my hand shakes
and distorts grainy memories
like sepia toned Polaroids

   a tad f u z z y   at the edges.

iii.

I grieve you
in the detached sorrow
that comes from acceptance

when, after standing too long
in a snowstorm,
you're suddenly aware of the cold.

iv.

this morning, I was examining
wounds left on my marred flesh,
experimenting with ink types
before the gashes could fully close.

it turns out,
even blood runs translucent
when I use it to write away your
memory on dried-out parchment

v.

removing your corpse one-handed,
I deposit you to the night

listening to wolves snarl
as they gorge themselves
on your remains
and I shiver,
wondering
what warm feels like.

Earth dies but we push on

this meadow grass forest stifles
rather than lightening my lungs;
the golden yarrow tilting flowering heads
in condolences as I brush past.

I stumble forward,
footfalls heavy
on untouched backwood floors.

the wagon I pull is more like rocks,
than the corpse of the small cria it cradles;
death has a way of making things
heavier than they are.

evening insects trill an eerie chorus of goodbye,
sounding the trumpets,
crickets summon the moon to begin its ascent.

everest and saffron hues
morph to ivory and ebony,
seeking to match the birch around them
as light succumbs to nothingness
in the passing of stolen clock hands.

the rut that held-fast my wheel
on the journey here,
bows out graciously on my return pass;

possibly understanding my need
for the quiet catharsis
of unencumbered walking.

back at the house,
there is this box of books I'm donating.
it's just sitting here outside the door.
they are getting rained on, and
all I can do
is watch the pages soak up the moisture,
curling at the edges
and get pissed off
that I'm too angry to care.

in the shed,
my old swiss army knife
cuts into paper grain bags
before I scoop out feed.
I mix by flashlight tunnel-vision;
steely in my resolve to make it to bedtime
before I break down.

but it's fucking hard,
when every gate sticks
and the small discovery of an
overturned water bin,
makes my tear ducts heavy.

not yet ready to venture into the darkness,
I put off retrieving the remaining alpacas
from the clutches of the night.
I stand at the open barn door
contemplating the rain;
how it's probably washing the maggots
off of her already decomposing skull,
in the place I laid her to rest
beside the bones of her mother.

what a strange and unforgiving
earth we live on.

*~Some farm days are hard, tonight took a toll on me, I had to lay to
rest the body of a one year old alpaca, only 6 months after her mother
died. Mother, Rapture, and daughter, Earth now rest together.*

The monsoon of his lament

Sorrow crept in,
an open contusion
the result of mixing things,
like lost time and summer rain.

A torrential downpour of
abandoned memories
washing over him,
like all the broken promises
and tethers
that lay cut and bleeding,
well laid plans
he buried
alongside her empty coffin.

A morning drizzle,
the first to touch
her misplaced body.
In his grief,
he envies the rain
for stealing her final embrace,
chilled as it may be.

Death comes, but you can't remember
if you said goodbye

I felt you today
pin pricks breezing
across my legs and forearms

I embraced the chill
as it washed over me

knowing,
you were saying goodbye

I keep catching myself
staring at nothing

waiting for something to happen

but life, in all its methodical glory
moves forward

so will I
when I can remember
to stop staring at dust motes
gathering on windowsills

Hookah Bar Nights

I had just finished
drying my eyes
from growing up to find that
love wasn't always enough,
when he slid in and
asked me to dance

he was beautiful
in a way I was unaccustomed to
like a piece of Italian pottery
fresh from the kiln and
his hands were too busy
tangled in my hair and
pressed on my hips
to care about the smoke stains
on my little black dress

I fell for him at Christmas
with cabernet from his family vineyard and
long California thunderstorms
the kind that are almost warm

my wild auburn curls and
thigh high boots drove him mad
so I danced naked
with my arms to the ceiling and
eyes on fire

in that grungy old apartment
while the pastor downstairs
smashed the floorboards
with his judgmental cane

he'd bring me lemon-drop martinis
and grin
as I ate up the karaoke stage
later, we'd grasp at each other's skin
like the world was ending

but march arrived and
dried up the music
wine bottles ran empty
rain forgot to be beautiful
and he forgot to love me

Moving forward

this landscape is changing
like the swatches of color
that dust the seasons of my life

there are places on the old oak
where the bark has worn off,
generations of children
using it as a passing point
to reach higher branches,
always something
more interesting ahead

those branches, now
decorated in an array of golds
with vibrant rust trimming,
a select few have already said their goodbyes,
lying as a grand blanket of sacrifice,
waiting in patient decay
for the icy breath of winter
to dress them in her bridal best

as the sun ages
my weary eyes find the horizon
with the acceptance of a warrior

my season here is coming to a close,
the next unknown,
but frost is nearly here
this evening was the last time
I'll tarry on the old bench in the grove,
writing beneath the tree fort
as my son climbs in youthful freedom

duty calls me elsewhere

gathering play buckets and
a child's ropes,
I take a small chilled hand in mine
and we trek back to the rickety farmhouse
sure of this,

our lives will always be an adventure
so long as I can hold his hand in mine

Nightshade

truth

My cloth cover

denoted to a stool,
I stand
three legged.

broken,
worn,
mimicking a smile.

setting softly
on the beaten floor,
the truth unravels

with undone stitches.

What's with trauma anyway

I hate that I forget my triggers
only to end up sobbing
when you ask if I'm ok

failing to back-trace the
moment I didn't measure up
in the fog-logged, scrambled eggs
beneath my skull

so here I am
    a mess
asking if you think I'm beautiful
even though I know your answer
    I think

there's a black hole
that lives in the far left corner
of our bedroom ceiling

it's spent hours feasting
scarfing up couplets and stanzas
like I starve it (I don't)

words flit off the page
    whirling
past my son's nightlight

bland colors
glancing off the curves
of runaway letters
to flash-blind me
before being sucked
into the void
vacuum-style

I dream in anime now, or
maybe this is just a Nyquil induced
hallucination
overacted and a tad too loud

these violent visions
are Miyazaki-worthy
watching the ones I love most
   die
against a stunning backdrop
in creatively horrific ways

     again
        and
          again

at least the cinematography is memorable

Mirage

i.

shallow lungs and impatient
rumbles fail at clearing murky sight
no experience in expanding senses
to lighten their desperate plight

ii.

even disparaging desert dunes
at peak resistance,
teem with manna
for the blind to scent

seekers mustn't be afraid of
sand-strewn trenches

iii.

amidst a mirage of sapling palms
the cactus remains when
dusk pockets pixels of daylight ire

iv.

when arid winds seek to
snuff out your roots,

remind them
you dine with their gods
when they come to fear your vision
offer them a seat at the table

that they might smell
a cacti's fruit
and dare to sliver open
heavily laden lids and wash sand
from dirty irises

v.

even desert storms
have a past they mourn,
the wind, given breath
in silenced shadows

Rise of the Autonomous

There is a great deception here,
a beast that controls the masses.
Do you see it?

There is a concept,
pushed to the edge of extinction:
Unconformity.
Passionate free thought.
The populous turn a blind eye,
too immersed in the search for conditional love
based in vanity and falsehoods.

Minds lobotomized
by the moguls and icons.
They have need of a resurgence of light,
an atomic flash to wake their sleeping cores.

Dangers lurk in every crevasse,
demanding recompense
for the lies uncovered, bit by bit.
But the uncontrolled will not give it to them,
we will fight back
with fire in our marrow
and dawn on our tongues.

The awakening is deception's greatest foe.

Beautifully wrapped fallacies

Sipping on the chorus of the blameless
spitting out the venom
of their lives.

These truths are fraught with perils,
the conscious Heimlich,
never gentle.

Best intentions in the tasting,
before the choke,
they went down sweet.

That's the thing
about most poison though,
the truth is in the meat

Buried Treasure

Winter's bones have chilled
and calcified my truths

this incessant blizzard
blanketing secrets

just above fossilized ferns
but beneath the permafrost

I'll not shovel out the snow
on this, the 93rd day of January

I find blow torches
far more appealing

let the fire sink in

Dandelion

Pyromania is the least of my problems

I can taste the promise
of an afternoon monsoon
on the sky's moist lips

the caress of electric current
builds against plateaus
of exposed flesh

I trust-fall into the onslaught
knowing there's soot under my nails

I've never been good
at cleaning up
after burning things

too often
relying on the rain
to wash me clean

Almost Sunrise

There is a forever
in my waiting
that is filled
with the melancholy
of yesterday

I think
I shan't
grant the power
it's demanding

denying it
the measly meanderings
of a never-ending day

nothing waits
for the iridescent
flippant side
of wanting

It simply
surges forward
powerful
within the absence
of everything
that's yet
to come

Torrential Acid

The clouds opened upon her as she fled,
water falling, like acid on her flesh
burning away any trace of her past,
melting the skin of repose,
opening the chasm of her being
until only bones remained.

A skeleton animated in the downpour,
bones clanking on weather-torn pavement
in steady staccato, they greeted the asphalt.

Lungs asphyxiated by the weariness of grief
and the sting of the cost of liberation,
she collapsed beside the road to her escape.

Limbs heavy beneath weight
of undesired existence,
her head fell to lull on trembling knees.

The drenching began to change.
A cool cascading flow moved to cover her,
a wave crashing into the unsuspecting shoreline.
The magnitude of the last few hours
stunning her into contemplative silence.

The late-afternoon Savanah rain,
slowly mending her open gashes.
Droplets, gingerly weaving silken thread,
sewing muscles and tissue seamlessly,
ensuing a brief glimpse of sunshine,
cast down upon her closed lids,
bathing her in the glow
of broken shackles.

First charred then mended by the storm,
she opens golden eyes to
welcome the sublimity of the setting sun.

The changing tides

yesterday,
now a millennia of days passed
plans were etched in granite,
a stoneware map
leading to a surrogate endgame

but kismet alterations
crushed carved stone,
creating a stunning mosaic
from the shards

rapid-fire lob dub, lob dub
shook me today
reality incinerating
what imagination
had tentatively painted of you

I was afraid to let you in,
to let you down

guarded, I wiped away
invented futures,
ideas that I once called dreams
were droplets of mist
next to the ocean of you

they lied to me,
let me believe you were a fantasy
I would never grasp

so I grieved the idea of you

and just as the dust of acceptance settled
on this crippled aorta
a surreal phenomenon stepped in,
a tiny Titan
ushering in an era of revolution

dormant possibility
measuring a mere three inches,
you are nothing shy of extraordinary

my miniature miracle
I live for you now

Hell must have a hell-of-a gym

I had sent my muse
on a recon mission years ago
and believed her dead

last week she showed up sopping wet
like she had been in a fist fight
with the ocean and came out swinging

her lithe frame,
a bit leaner and sharper edged
than I remember,
sported a black eye
and torn chemise

once petite plumage had grown
draping heavy, past bare ankles
long ebony feathers trailing in her wake

she smoothly plucked a quill from
between her shoulder blades
as an archer would draw from his quiver
the head, dripping crimson from the tear

she placed it between my fingers as
my inkwell clinked on my bedside table,
filled with the saltwater
she'd been retrieving these past two years

dipping the tip to the well
blood mixed with the sea
and she sighed
as I scrawled those first words

Bloodied hands

final filament shorn
a bedraggled puppet
drew its last breath
decamping this plane in pieces
a new creature arose
to claim the broken form

from the shadows she departed
oozing contusions
smeared 'cross old birth-lines
altering her identity as
vermillion crusted over flesh

flames stirred beneath
a dying veneer
shedding the final ashes
as sand to line her path

dipping a toe
into the firmament of
who she might become
she let loose her thunderstone
and joined the wind
in a taunt

Azalea

healing

Muddied shades of gray

In my naïveté
I once lived
in the simplicity
of black and white

my alabaster past
painted in a coat of coal
and I, rebelled
with soot covered knees,
lighting fires,
just to stave off
the residue of ash

as years peeled away
I acquainted myself
in the multiplicity
of sleet gray sheets

filling in both sides
of the pendulum,
inky shades
and translucent swatches
convulsed in convoluted intricacies

mucking up pristine
ivory ideals
with beautifully tainted
muddy work boots
and fire singed
coat tails

In my naïveté
I once lived
in the simplicity
of black and white

Denouncing debilitating debris

i.

these years conditioned my hands,
like a master wood smith
I have perfected the craft
of sanding down uncalled images

I flip a switch,
rough paper swiftly
distorting flashbacks
and tuning out
supposedly deleted scenes

they come so rarely now
triggered by a smell usually,
residual markers
of cognizant recognition

it's always the little things

ii.

I thought I had it handled.
my wounds,
merely faded scars,

but beneath the skin,
hidden in the murk
of my subconscious,
the residue of pain
still festered

unrealized,
unnamed

I fought it,
buried it
nearly forgot it

but there it sat
patiently waiting
to be given a voice
yet I denied it...
not realizing,
that like a cancer
it fed on my fear

iii.

you gave it a voice,
drawing from the darkness
phantoms I didn't know
lay subdued,
lacerations languidly oozing

together, we turned back the clock,
examined skeletons of the monsters
that have plagued us

finally liberating me
from the shared past
I had thrown a veil over

iv.

I felt the shift in the cosmos.

there was a moment
when it rushed me,
an energy field
invading this essence
only to wash over me in
reverberated waves of peace

v.

strange, this feeling,
like a weighted blanket hovering
over skin stretched too-tight

the release,
a euphoric levitation
of changing frequencies

the shaky remnants of
dead demons being scourged
from pores that bleed black
for the last time

shades eradicated
at long last

this craft-smith
has shelved my sander,
stowing its paper in the back drawer

hopefully it gathers dust there

Remembered identities

i.

my Midas-touch is defective,
baring loss in gain's stead.
even my once green-thumb is
dappled in deep mauve bruises;
plants pale and wither
under my nurturing tutelage.

ii.

a fingertip's graze,
marks tiny treasures for doom;
placing on them,
an invisible inking

calling from the darkness,
a black hole to engulf them.

save yourself from me.

iii.

around the corner,
a tiny hand fills mine
and I am reminded what I am.

my soothing embrace
permeates the barriers of fear.
the mere brush of my lips
shatters the thresholds of pain,
and in the ebb and flow of his tears,
I become the savage
his monsters fear.

iv.

relinquished innocence reclaimed,
I join my son in a wild game of chase;
dodging lightning under a midday downpour.

v.

I am magic;
wielding it tenaciously,
I dress his days
in warm rainstorms
and finger-painted mosaics.

forget gold-cursing Greek gods,
I am magic

Memoirs of a caged bird

in a house on a hill
the meadow lark hordes memories

pinecones and branches
crumpled from abuse

plumage
nurtured beneath the wings
of rusted shutters and picked paint

the entrance boasted faulty locks
broken hinges and weathered
window frames

still,
even revolving doors
hold little consequence
when the lark is missing feathers

there were a few pulled and
abandoned in each room

littering open floor space
gathering dust

plucked nearly bare,
she held inside a song

that might shatter shutters and
dry the fountains that weep

her feathers,
like a children's game
of hidden treasures,
can be found in unexpected places

a few plucked in the old tree house,
left to decompose
alongside fallen comrades
in the back wood

some,
strewn carelessly behind the barn,
in waking midnight mourning

each quill pulled
elicited a silent wail
but buried deep inside
a longing song of sorrow

waiting for the lark to dip
into the ink and find her voice

dull, dirty and damaged plumage,
sewn with black widow's
tenacious silk,
dawned a different bird

it was a storm
that finally brought her voice,
one like never seen prior

gone was the tender lark,
taking heed from Icarus,
an albatross opened
refurbished wings

and sang in flight,
ever wary of the lying sun

Iris
hope

Oil paint on a sharp tongue

I cracked a book today,
it laughed at me

that I dared deem myself versed
in the intricacies of pain

'so naïve' it mocked

I held it open,
consumed in yellowed pages
I deliberated as to why
shadows thrive
like malignant growths
on youthful arteries,
when they should wither
in the serene alkaline stasis
of this brooding aorta

change is scarcely ushered in
through docile encounters
no, it's blood and fire
that give rise, when fate
compiles her preordained chapters

    so I burned the book

and turned to the budding bloom
of cerulean-tinged flames,
warming my hands as deft fingers
sewed up my study of sorrow's depths

embracing the etymologist in me
I'll narrate a virgin compendium,
the refrain of love's simplistic embers
call out to me from the darkened alleys
where I once resided

though, the complexities
feel more like undefinable hues,
than syllables to be pinned in place

perchance my brush
would better paint your likeness
than my traitorous tongue
could spell you into form

I'll construct a palette
to hold your colors
from the ashes
of my burnt thesaurus

and enjoy the irony of its make-up,
only picky, when it comes to oils

Madness is a matter of perspective

haunted, slate-grey eyes plead
reverting into agonized slits,
echoes of defeat
carved into marrow

pint-sized pink toes curl and pull up
knees bent in matching desperation

shrieks slice through weary bone
to spring free the hands
of an iron clock that doesn't chime

foreign hues reside outside blurred lines,
furniture shadows
etched in raw, fluid crayon

gradually slipping,
I cling to sanity
walls crumbling around me
clutching at bits
they disintegrate into embers
dancing
before a metal owl's sunflower-eyes
in ebony silence
her mocking gaze pierces through wails
to condemn my tired tears

climbing steps on autopilot
resignation fades into flashes of misplaced anger,
guilt settling in just as swiftly

    tonight I span the spectrum

slivers of chocolate
melt between warm lips
playing at the fringes of lucidity

vacant stares numbly observe
his full-body spasms
shaking me from this comatose
I'm vaguely aware of wet cheeks,
the result of a sporadic empathy leak

    4am crisp air
    hits naked flesh
    this is a type of 'awake'
I guess
    in the same way
    ventilation is breathing
    a pained excuse
    that doesn't quite live up to the hype

words don't come quickly to me anymore

maybe it's the sleep deprivation
or maybe just my inability to find poetry
inside things that don't hurt

these colored pencil scribbles
overrun one another
letters bleeding together
no one to blame but the darkness

swaying in the starkly lit living room
to the tune of a song
that makes me momentarily forget
the extent of my fatigue

nestled close, the crying ebbs
the corners of his tiny innocent mouth
turning up just slightly,
liquefying my insides
with wide, trusting eyes

a pearl of revelry sneaks in
embedding itself into the canvass of this
ceaseless witching hour
a beacon driving me on

When gas is $5/gallon, but I can't
breathe

why is it always raining
when the concept of giving up
slinks into my vision
in bold print

I'm drinking myself back to sanity
or into oblivion
not really sure which
    then again
espresso will only take me one of those places
and I'm too tired
for the headache alcohol brings

butted up against a cold city wall
trying to decipher why it's called red brick
when it's not red

the mixture of blue and green with
bits of orange tinged in black
stares back at me accusatorially

I give it the middle finger
like that crazy cat lady who talks to herself
and stick it in reverse`

self-medicating with
highly caffeinated sugar and
wasted gasoline
I flee the city
driving till I can feel
the trees' spindly fingers
reaching out to pull me in

I pull off Plum School Road
into a field where semi cabs go to die
and I slide into park
allowing myself to fall into a daze
mesmerized by the way
the oaks nestle themselves
into the hillside

marshland lies to my left
open fields to my right and
a silo before me
vines crisscrossing up its time-ravaged husk
like the veins in my lungs
fighting each other for the privilege
of bragging rights to decomposition

a discarded couch upside down and
half pulled apart
sits next to the road and I feel a kinship to it
I pull out and move on
past where the pavement ends and

the skies seem to stretch
like the old country songs
that I only listen to alone

taking winding gravel slowly
I make turns without agenda
until one calls me to pull off

the rain pelting the windshield
I watch a pair of geese
dance around each other
beside a lake
I don't know the name of

I sip my drink
breathe in the
chilled, damp air
letting the radio mix with geese calls,
notes rolling across my chest and
feel the strings begin to loosen

Self-portrait

I have my mother's burnt sienna irises,
her proportioned curves and generous thighs,
her small wrists and gentle heart

my father gifted me
the small dimple in my chin
and that indent in just one cheek,
the one I always tried to hide.

I inherited his mother's wild auburn curls.
they take enjoyment in pissing me off,
tight spirals on one side and loose
on the other
like my son took a scissors
to my sleeping head,
leaving me lopsided.

I also stole my father's height,
towering over friends in grade school,
but my grandmother
always told me to stand tall,
head high, shoulders back...

so I wore heels,
just to say, 'F you'
to the insecure boys who'd
called me a giant.

my heels are retired now,
no need to prove a point.

I used to pair long V-necks
with short jean skirts,
a pained attempt to draw eyes
to the body I thought was all I was,
unaware my smile was worth far more
than their leering looks.

these days
I only change from farm clothes
to dress in my sexist work uniform.
made to wear a short black skirt,
I rebel and pair it with leggings

   my 'F you' to the boss-man

beside my heart, 'gypsy' is scribed
scrolling letters with tips almost
touching gothic wings
that spread 'cross shoulder blades,
curling in artful twists,
black lines wisp down my spine,
seeping outward like feathered fingers

   tributes to the wanderer
   that always felt lost.

my once enviably flat stomach
is missing the sparkling trinket
that hung from it years ago.
it's softer now, riddled with lines,
a war ground of grandeur.
I proudly wear my battle scars,
proof of my greatest accomplishment,
the son I was told
I might never be able to carry.

my body,
a hybrid of bloodlines,
but I am so much more than
a mixture of DNA
or the pixels of some picture.

it took me years
to at last see me,

the one the glass forgot existed,
the one who used to 'force' that smile,
the one who sees how beautiful
this sometimes cruel world is

who knows that breaking mirrors
is just the beginning.

Magnolia

love of nature

Utterance in time

i.

shunned,

in weighted turmoil
rolling gray of elemental suffocation
buried me
in years, lying dormant

trapped in ice sheets
my echoes digressed to
bubbles through cracks
of a tempered glacier

ii.

subdued,

waiting in eager submission
drops ping as chimes
on defrosting surfaces

a quiet opus
takes root,
shoots, begotten by ill intent
through bated hungry negligence
rise defiant, to sing

iii.

wild,

carnivorous vines seek limbs
to climb,
slithering 'cross warm flesh
my pores seep dew, to tunes
of unrecognized birdsong

growth set to fast forward,
I'll catch my breath tomorrow

iv.

unraveling,

cyclones submerge
in torrents of sweet retreat
chill embraces my fevered forehead
carrying promises of bleak,
colorless aftermath

respite
from the burden
of failing to paint
colors of virtue

v.

unbound,

I unleash a chasm
of wordless retort

restraints removed
syllables clash,
merging into the void

returning,
in violent fervor
screaming blue lines
on yellow pages

scribbles, ease the ache

vi.

a paragon of incoming bonfires, my warm tones
descend in wavering supplication, watercolors
painted with the vibrato of my vocal cords, where
ominous violins mark notes of my passage, let our
gypsy feet dance to the tempo of chilling thunder.

Tranquil mornings

it's an eerie lullaby,
the song of death

a waking star stretches,
her fingertips break the horizon
roving to the jolting tune
of coyotes heartily feasting
far too close

pale purple lilacs,
bereft of their usual butterfly cloak,
shift abruptly
churning air,
the effect of gunshot rounds
littering the woodland floor

quiet studiously returns

The irony of warmth

I find a thrill
in the chilled caress
of frigid summer mornings

much in the same way
I detect beauty
hidden in inky depths

there is something infatuating
in the gift of the unexpected

Shrine to the red maple

the 8:00 am birthing
of a midday star
reaches a solitary blushing sapling
surrounded by mature conifers

her colors, emboldened
by the stark contrast
of too-soon powder and
late morning amber beams

vermilion and magenta
slosh as a full-bodied merlot
against richly shaded
green hemlocks and the
blinding whites of
an over-eager winter courtship

a passionate teenager,
she stands in rebellion
flushing in tones of fuchsia
refusing to accept frozen vapors
that come to rest
on her dying leaves

beside a peacocking aspen's
vibrant mustard morsels,
premature crystals

are readily absorbed into
a thirsty young maple's
blood-orange veil

the tree's wilting fingers
demanding one final drink
before surrendering
to the journey
of an autumn breeze

October snowfall
shouldn't be whiteout,
but a menagerie
of warm tones
flitting gracefully up from
birch and oak forests
to pirouette before a
blue-gray backdrop

the hair follicles of a sapling
enthralling a backlit gaze,
catching light
as they cartwheel
'cross a gravel footpath

challenging January precipitation
for the honor of a queen's crown

inhaling spicy fir,
the unique scent signature
of the soft evergreen army
that will protect her virtue
against a vile and demanding December

she cries a droplet of sap,
not yet made sweet by time
and surrenders
the last of her clothing
to a rare, warm zephyr
eyes tight, her branches bare,
she listens to the voice of the forest
as it calls its child home

Glazed over

no breeze
on stagnant air
this morning

a lack of zephyrs
to inspire
changing moods

therefore

melancholy
is the way
I'll start my day

no bright sunrise
to lend a refreshing palate
to cascade over me

just heavy
monochromatic skies
and multifaceted gloom

encumbering me
in gray

Urban trance

twilight's bloom wanes,
    easing us into the silky warmth
of an early September eve

how I've longed for the
  far-flung transparency
of the desolate wild

to loiter as dust
    against an unbound
spread of star clusters,

or be nestled into the
    cerulean haze
of a rouge nebula

but light pollution's stamp
    is the solitary murk
this town concedes to me

so tonight, I'll withdraw
    to my dossier of star-capped hills
and bathe in vagary's kiss

indulging in the striking reflection
    of a meteor shower
glancing off Lake Superior's glassy face

Nature: my drug of choice

i.

popping Tylenol like tic-tacs
but the headache won't budge
in my tilt-a-whirl world

like a middle school chalk board
fingernails scrape the underside
of my eyelids
the sound only perceptible
inside my skull

scraaaaaatttcccchhh
now that's a new way to go insane

ii.

windshield wipers blur
to match the fuzzy reflection in
my rear view mirror

a line of bare trees
wear burnt orange petticoats
just around their midriffs
flashing their knobby knots like
exposed breasts that got too cold
and hardened into driftwood

I can't recall whether this poem
is supposed to be happy
        or sad
just lost inside the painful beauty
that is nature's wrath

iii.

I pass Crooked Creek rd where the
tractor lines have filled with rainwater
turning soil to muck
the raccoon bobble head on my dash
nodding along in approval

god I love storms

iv.

melting snow reveals
just how many deer carcasses
were left behind by winter's icy hold

a word to the wise
never read poetry
while drinking tea and
driving two-fingered
in the rain

the deer will never forgive you

v.

I'm not a painter
but my fingers itch for a brush
and oils to blend
with a deft urgency
as I drive through art
that breathes

it's the weeping willow
resembling an old timey
Dr. Seuss character
that makes my eyes glassy

gangly and misshapen
like a tall, frumpy ballerina
that's off-balance
and wearing yesterday's clothes

her saturated yellow dreadlocks
a-bit-too-thin to be cool
stand guard at a moss covered
stone entryway where
nature has begun to take back a
crumbling nineteenth century redstone

vi.

witnessing the first signs of spring
in the rich green grass
under a steel gray sky
the pillowy tops of cotton balls
breaking through in the distance
chopped off and underlined in cobalt blue

tree trunks burst from the water
roots submerged
greedily drinking the icemelt that
proved too much for the riverbank

crossing over the bridge to nowhere
I stare down at the black ripples and
watch the breeze shift
through the dried grasses
that are overgrown beside the road

it's the tufted heads of marsh grass
that held to the stalk
through the slow frigid months
that wave to me

I feel alive again

vii.

I slow to pass a horse and buggy
and roll my windows down
to hear the sheep bleating on the crisp air
fresh from the rain

viii.

when red sports cars are parked
beside red barns
next to the one room school building
that says K-12

I know I'm almost home

Monkey Face Orchid

humor and oddities

A good challenge is hard to resist

I have never played cheerleader
to dull intentions
always drawn to the next adventurous tease,
these wanderlust feet getting
anxious after standing too long...
nervous that roots
might accidentally take hold

a shrink would likely blame
my detachment issues,

ha!
my demons are darker than that.
or maybe they aren't
and I just don't like boring

loving fiercely for brief moments
dancing on the coals,
my inner gypsy sending breath
to snuff the flames

perhaps someday,
I'll throw some trick candles
her way

good luck blowing those out bitch

Well hello there

For all that is good and Holy,
I sit here and chuckle to myself
as I compile poems for this book.
Knowing someone in my family
is bound to buy it
and be absolutely appalled
by the depravity, language,
and sexual content.

I'll go back to being the black sheep
that I was at 13,
when I grew too fast for my clothes,
and double D's and tight shirts
made me a bad influence.

Or when I was 18 and
moved out from under my rock
to live on the West Coast
and decided alcohol-fueled nights,
cigarette breath and full back tattoos
were the new me.

when that lesbian joke
I made about Angelina Jolie on
good ol' MySpace,
was a little too much

for the ultra conservatives.

It's not like any of this behavior
could've been a cry for help
from a kid
who was more lost than found,
but don't worry
I turned out just fine.

If you're reading this,
I forgive you.
We've all had a little bit
of *fucked up*
embedded into our childhoods
and adults need healing too.

The world isn't always butterfly dreams
and papier-mâché hearts.

When the weather lets you down

my mood is supposed to predict
the elements
but everything my eyes touch
is disgustingly breathtaking

pure morning light
hits changing leaves before they fall,
morphing red to vibrant rust

it kisses the dew on
 honeyed grass in overgrown pastures

making me want to destroy something.

maybe I'll pick photography back up,
snap a few award-winning shots,
just so I have something epic for kindling

fuck sunrises

Even the night sky is jealous of the
whims of a butterfly

a quaking chrysalis unfurls,
her supple sprawling form
awaits euphoria's reach

bedding down on silk and muslin
she beckons constellations

a celestial abandons his place
in the stratosphere
heeding her aphonic roar

starlight in his gaze
he burns for her
as they crest the
chasm of space entwined

deft fingers
embolden her tongue

unfettered,
    her voice
        melts suns

That little voice inside me
needs reading material

Disclaimer:
    I am a little too much
    HOT'nNOW cheesy potato bites and
    not enough hippy-ass smoothies

    so I switched to less sugar in my coffee
    and I can already tell
    I'm going to be a bitch today

you know when you read something good
like really good
and you can feel the needle enter the vein
heroin-style
opening the release valve
to an IV of caffeine

your blood pumps just a touch faster
hairs standing on end, in salute
and you start seeing things
you're not sure
were there before

I want that

to be spellbound at dusk
rolling into slumber
to dream in the voice of Homer's pen
and wake with a poem on my tongue

not a big ask

Evensong

she evades worlds
with desolate abandon
her steps unmeasured
save by disciples
lost in veneration
her unfiltered sacrament
a sapid morsel to a dying star

ever satiated
yet methodical in hunger
she baits lattice with gossamer allure
entangled in a melodious web
her seraphic tongue unintentionally
enthralls another shooting star
adding to her collection
of hoarded wishes
cast upon a deadly lullaby

the sultry revolt of our delight
sinuously sinful
playful in reckless abuse of self-imposed purgatory

this composite of starlight
our last stand
against the synthetic archetypes
of a fatally wounded universe
the army she's amassed

rise from bended knee
staccato ascent into a
cacophony of primal revolution

their battle
an epic light show
in a waning evening sky
sacrificing all
she is immortalized
in a spectacular constellation
an ethereal reminder
of the cost of dreams

Fallen

his gaze descends as snowflakes
thousands of icy flecks
melting to summer rain
as they land on my warm expanse

is he a destroyer
clothed in an archangel's vellum
or a savage savior
masked in the flesh of a deity

nay
he is a world-ender
an epic plague
poison or the elixir
I know not

still
I empty my bottle of him
the final drops
tingling on my tongue

a surge of power
coasts the fevered veins of a
vessel previously thought broken

resolute that his presence
is the beginning of my end

I succumb to the inferno
of complete surrender
masterful lips
destined to kiss the fiery dawn
in a glimpse of vulnerability
find mine instead

closing lids over lethal irises
he embraces the fall
choosing the taste
of my velutinous embrace
over the enticing aroma
eternity offers

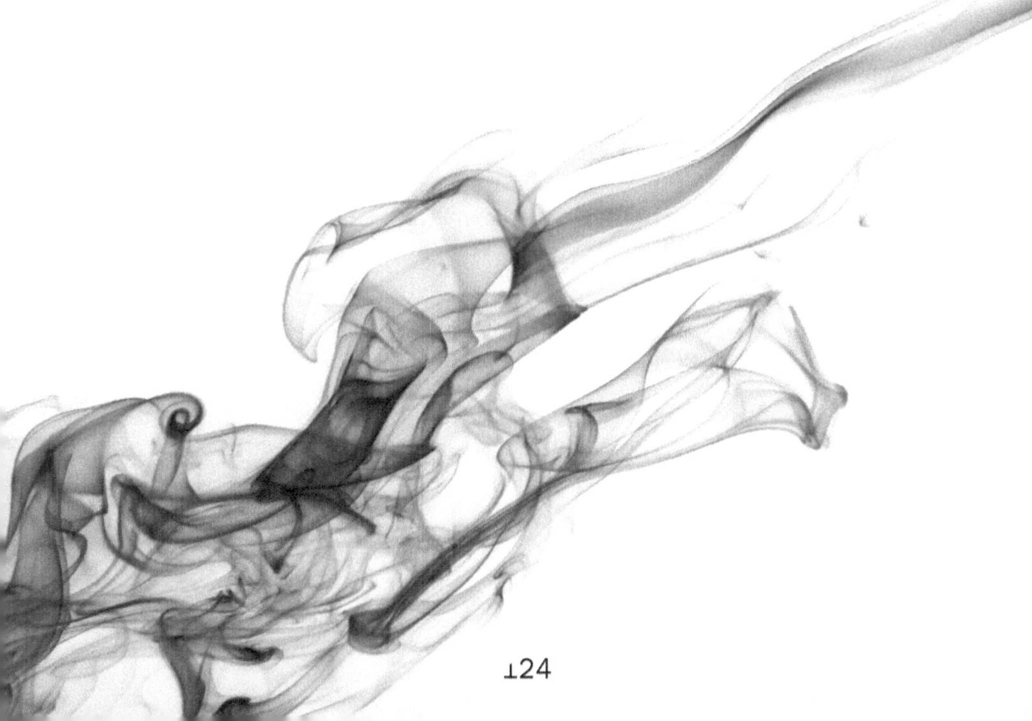

Unearthing amnesia

will I watch in contained glee
as I exhume the remains
of what once was me

will I recognize the curvature
of my fossilized jawline
     or
with my peers
will I study the architecture
of anciently strewn relics;
attempting to glean a glimpse
into countless winters long-fled

a millennia from now,
will I recollect my prehistoric aura
purging lives lived in the interim
as memories fade with births
the way color abandoned the
foliage that covered me

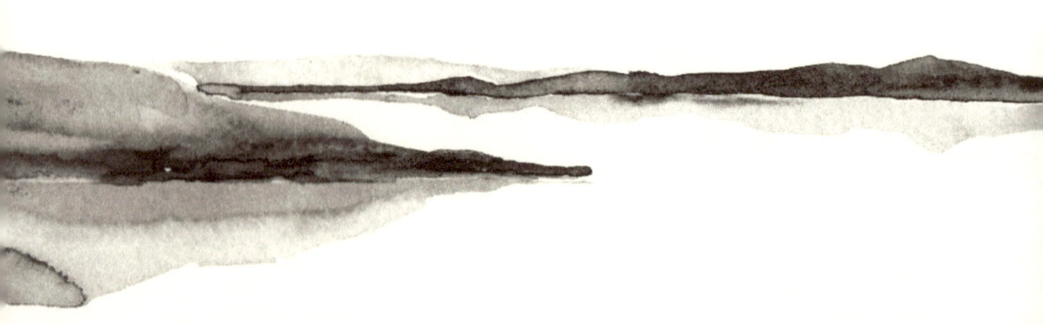

will long buried words
come surging back at
our primal connection,
echoes carried through
the passage of time
to rock the fiber of my being

will I breathe me in
until I remember me

or will I hover above the scene
watching it unfold
and gently laugh
at the simplicity
of the fractured human psyche

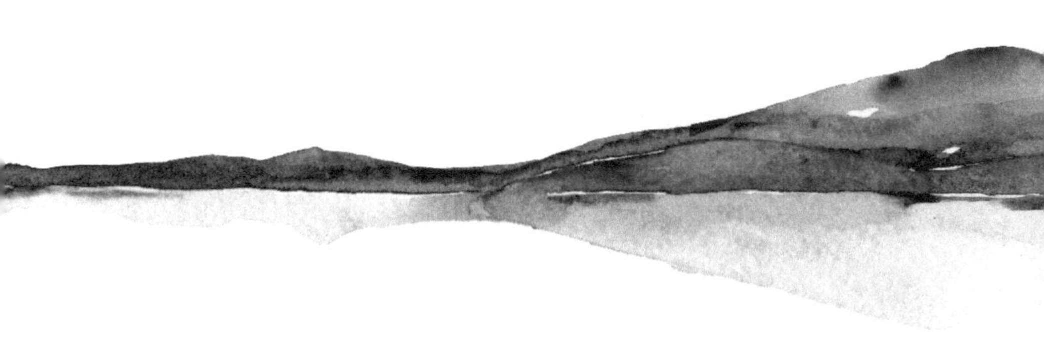

Guardian Archer

rise up!

shake loose the collar
of your compulsory torment
obliterate the yoke

break free, the nullified contract
set fire to cowardice
rain ashes down
upon raging canine predators
as you chant your battle cry

your arrows,
skillfully crafted
to upend the nefarious

so notch your bowstring
make ready your echo
run from predatory safety
bring the fight
to the their darkened gates

bear your talismans into battle
rupture the phantasm of enmity
let the false face of duality slough off
        a molting,
like the skin of our resurrection

let flow, the river of forgiveness
cascading over broken dams
and rotted trees that struggle to restrain it

embrace healing
in a deluge
of elemental stimulation

befriend the giver
calling forth
gentle rain
from your clouded covering.

when the storm clears
after the battle and
the crisp bite to the air signals
you're not done

rise up!

Power outages in my head

there is blood in my poetry
the kind that seeps
from self-inflicted wounds
to drip, in taunting rivulets
as viscous ink

marring the ivory
of my zygomatic arches

slow and meaningless

I can taste the copper
at the corners of my lips
where you kissed
away my torment

slipping on wet tiles
we grind with clumsy symmetry
our labored breaths vibrating
the walls of vacant, lightless halls

your possessive fingers
purple my hipbones
in frantic urgency

only for us to slide
'cross the chilled slab
of this heimal
wasteland

where black ice
trips over itself
and permafrost
lies dormant

the February thunderstorm
subsides into a rush of heady cologne
and warm undertones

Infiltrated sleep

he was a twister of light, a thief
who mastered surface dances
in shrouded glee

succinctly unaware of a
birth taken place in the darkness

the Nuada dragon
risen amid turmoil
exhales cerulean crystals
an icy sword
penetrating the veil of
our indoctrination

a grand libretto,
sedately serenading
war-blinded masses

examining fear at its dawn
intoxicating us in the
bosom of truth amidst captivity

~Cliamh Solais also call "the Sword of Light" in Celtic folklore, was wielded by the Irish god of Justice and Truth. The sword was a glowing silver blue, like the icy breath of a dragon.

It's a coffee and f-bombs kind of day

tangling in the brambles
shadows
like Death's wispy extremities
fragile and bony

dance out to grasp at my hair
dry rot seeping in at the edges
grotesque and looming
they reach down
to make a play for me

while an upside-down Jackal is
playing the blues
from my ceiling,
giving me the stink eye
in-between howls

   and I kinda like it

but I'm just creeped out enough
not to ask for an encore

   now let's take a moment
   to sit inside the dark chasm
   that is melancholy
   and pretend that we are poets

breathing in the memories
our words spin into yarn
like the oxygen
we know them to be

the jackal's back
this time he's wearing a malefic grin and

lounging disheveled on my bed
quietly strumming away
to the tune of baby shark
until I chuck my lumpy pillow at him
and down some melatonin with an edible

maybe now he'll go away
and my teeth will stop falling out
bloody in my dreams
while I cup my mouth
gumming the silence

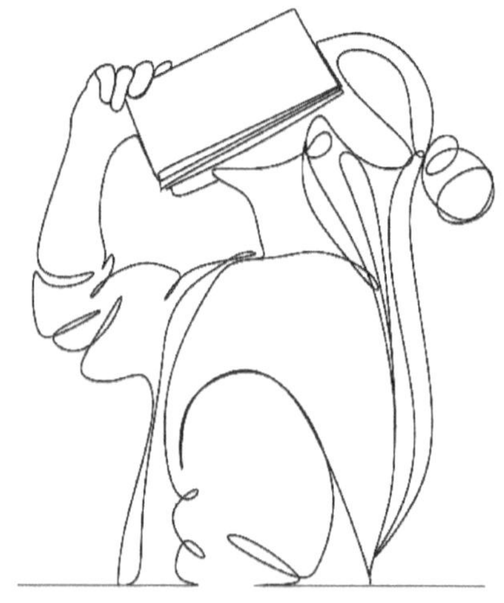

Pink Camellia
longing

Empty afternoons

an early morning mist
traces the gentle curves
of hyacinth petals
as they seek to bloom
under its weight

outplaying the sweet kiss
of midnight dew
that stretched high
in hopes of bewitching
wildflowers into a dance

like that dew
memories of a past
not yet lived
sometimes settle on me
on empty afternoons

you are always there
teasing me
with midnight rain while
whispers lent of
secret rendezvous
grant my reluctant grin

when someday you find me
bewitch this bloom into a dance
trace my essence with
the mist of your warm breath
rise with me all the mornings

Auroras in Nod

a heliotrope sunset alluringly purrs
peach and coral at its parting
treetop skeletons aimlessly stir
serenaded by Sol's whispered ballad

this decrepit barn's modest overhang
is a paltry umbrella from flakes
liquefying on my phone screen

layers that once began to melt
are now fixed in an inverted arc
precariously suspended off the eve
taunting me

shades of indigo and muted lilac
engage in an early February duel
as regiments of arctic rain catch
the hint of a lingering lambent aria
igniting the evening sky
like firefly glitter
floating to me
on remnants of a frigid zephyr

reminding me
that sunshine
is often stifled

lost inside miles
of witching hour gloom

with each eventide apart
nyctalopia penetrates my lids
and I'm left
ever searching
for the rays you've woven
into the dark corners
of my dreams

the Romans had it right

like ancient Aurora,
I don my nimbus with a smirk
tipped to the side
you nudge it back in place
with the curve of your lips

conjured from my
overactive imagination,
your goddess of the dawn
I masquerade in darkness

primordial halo
cast on jagged rocks
eons before I honed the
art of artificial happiness

yet, the grin I grant you
can't recall wings that bled out
leaving the residue of
inky feathers on my flesh

it knows only
the aura my skin oozes
at your demanding touch

say I'll be your Eos
I'll wear you like a crown

vibrational vapor
ceding to my touch
I surrender
into the addiction
of your esoteric command

The mask I wear

i.

I have a penchant for bad things,
at least I used to

no longer,
can I pull days
from shored up black blanks

my mind
holding only bricks and mortar
"authorized access only"

time has a way of
skewing memories

ii.

those who loved me,
were the ones I released
back to the tempered sea

perpetually in fear
of being alone
yet,
I shunned the ones who
begged to stay

iii.

I ran
it was always the story
if it felt right,
felt safe,

I fled
before it could decimate me

that,
or sometimes boredom found me
in the unfamiliar warmth
that came with security

my wild side always too
restless to love

iv.

there lies a safety now
in my loneliness
so I cling to it
in the way
that I used to embrace the wild

the only way I know how
with every fiber of my hollow core

v.

there will always be pieces missing
likely scattered to far off ocean tides,
a poet's lungs are made to breathe
or are they meant to suffocate?

I always get the two mixed up

vi.

loneliness is a mask I wear only
in stolen moments, and
boredom hasn't been used to
describe my world in years

but or rare nights, when
zephyrs settle on my bare toes,
I don that faded mask,
basking in my secret rebellion

Contused dawns between us

I wake this morning, sore
a night spent in labored slumber
my very bones reaching out
but you, my home, are waiting
biding time, in my absence

there is a failure to thrive
inside this famine of you
my grip, always grappling
stretching 'cross miles
to run fingertips over flesh

this drought is draining
I call on your thunderstorm
in the midst of building heat
seek out your manna
in this raging desert storm

your murmur soothes racking aches
yet these hands clutch at cold sheets
lonely for the warm frame they call home

Ossature of daydreams

as a crow, evicting itself from
naked, skeletal aspen limbs
writing in the wake of a graphite dusk
with what colors will you paint me
when the sun enacts her suicide dive

blind
will you recant placements of
changing hues adorning your palette,
painting my likeness
with the blameless brush of
a perfect copy artist

I'd rather you cling
to stygian oceans,
be led to delve
into arcane oil splotches
with closed irises

to simply
    feel me

I yearn be painted fluorescent
ruddied flesh bathed in coral
cobalt locks ablaze in wind-torn freedom
my lilac lashes cresting a piceous stare

paint me on a backdrop of the night sky
that I might befriend the constellations
a breath before we join them

if someday
your battered boots grace
the blades I walk on,
gift me this

or do I ask too much

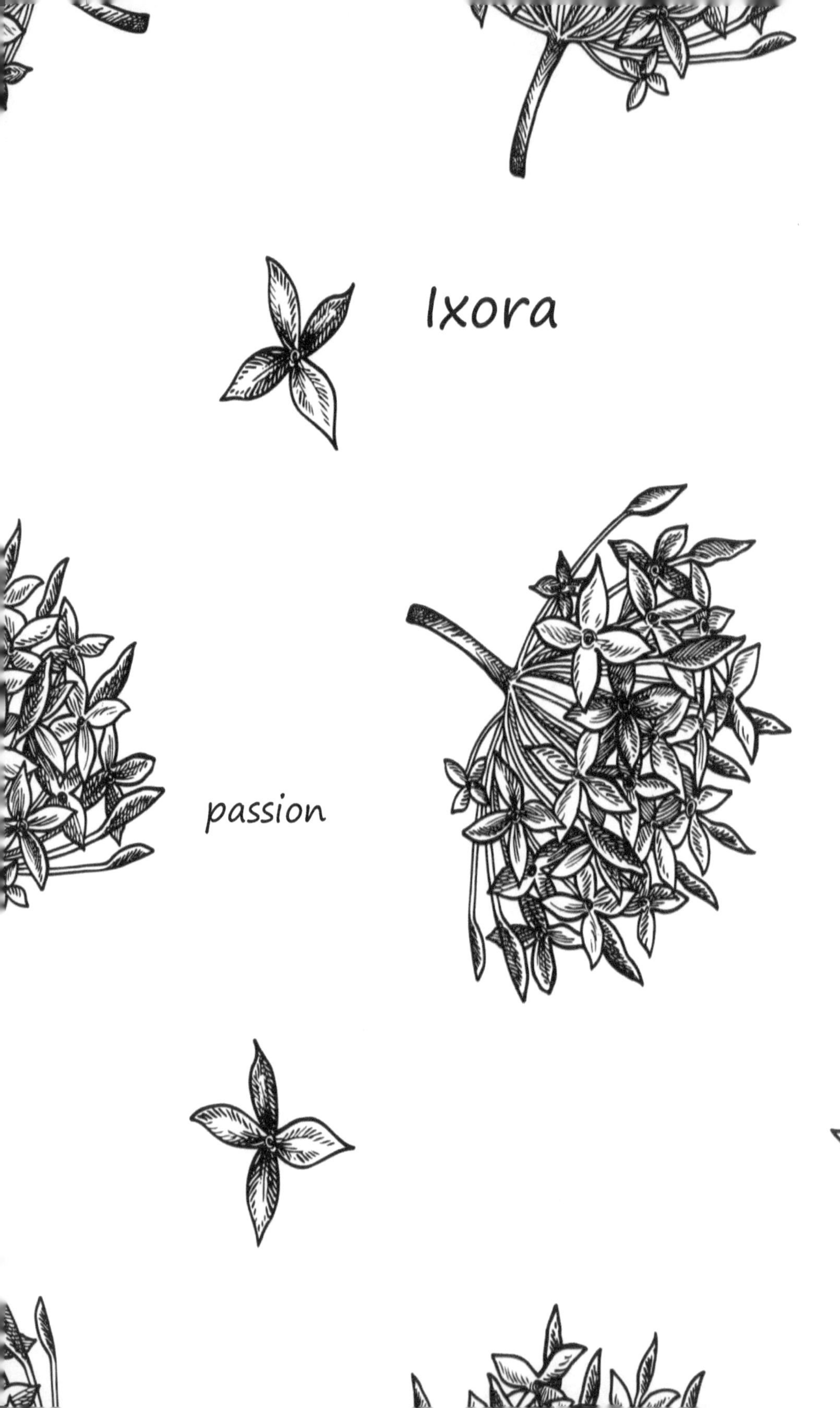
Ixora
passion

Caught in your trap

You love like a repentant villain,
unmasked and paraded through
the shadows of the night,
paying homage to me
like I'm the recompense you desire for eternity.

I breathe in your kiss like a raging storm,
effervescent, utterly destructive
in the deepest hours devoid of light,
denied absolution by the guardian of my heart.

Grant me your touch thief,
that I may bask in the aftermath
of our intimate annihilation.
Tuck me inside the river of your essence,
I will bathe in the thrills
of love's bittersweet revolt.

The remnants of our broken pieces
meld together with intricate precision.

Many a night I woke,
the unknown image of you
vanishing just before I grasped it.
My dreaming soul,
peeking at memories
of a past lurking in tomorrow's dawn.

Ambrosia junkie

I'm sure there have been many
who's thighs your charms have unlocked,
countless inches of cream and caramel skin
you've explored before tasting mine

forecasting amnesia in your future,
I've laced my milk with poison
just enough to get you hooked
but if you pray for an overdose
I won't deny you

worship me
in the vermillion and lavender
of our sunrise addictions

I'll play doctor to your ailing lungs
on early September mornings

my shattered breath as antidote,
forget all yesterday's before me
inside the delirium of our tangled dawn

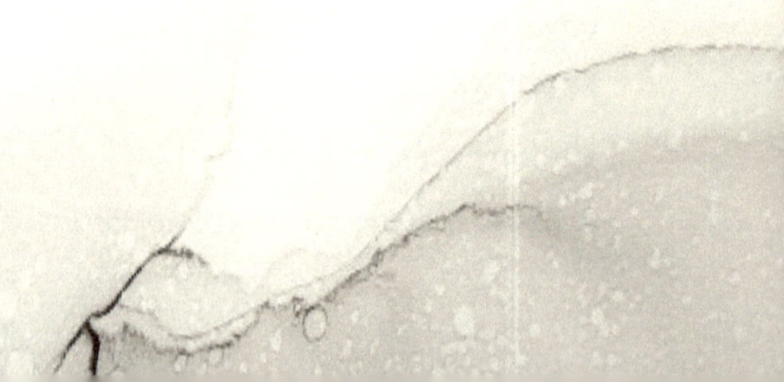

Broken timepiece

with the ticking clock
as our enemy
and the miles between us,
his weapon of choice

we seek solace in
stretching stolen days
learning one another
between gasped inhales

vesting to the recesses
of memory,
the intricacies of
contrasting skin tones
and the intensity of
ancient ties, exposed

Confessions

what if I told you
I wanted to taste
the tequila on your lips

to gently torment the soft
tissue of your neck, trace
teasing grazes below your ear

I might let on
that haunted onyx eyes
have captured me

you make me
want to be vulnerable
just to test your somber strength

fully clothe myself in satin
to better enjoy
your lurid undressing

I'll have you for my masseuse
that every muscle might be
touched by inked up fingers

to inhale the ferocity
of obsidian midnights and
pen your symbols onto my skin

I'm aware the power words wield
I am their sorceress
conjuring you to my touch

I want to taste words
unspoken, on swollen lips
that beg to be ravaged

to call your beast
and let you loose
to embrace your wild

I am no fragile flower
no delicate submissive
to be broken on a whim

I am the witching-hour wind
that spurs you forward
the storm that rides you till dawn

I am freedom
if only,
for a night or two

Tangible sunrises

darkness yields to daylight,
ushering in a budding warmth
riding the sun's coattails

you catapult me into A-fib,
no stethoscope needed
to hear my erratic beats

I lie here waiting,
bleeding sunsets
so that you might tend
to my aching skin,
your practiced touch
cauterizing my wounds
into early morning hours

I'd like to try my hand at a mallet,
tapping ever so lightly

on that gossamer-coal crust
you've encrypted 'round your chest cavity,
see if it might crack just a bit
at my not-so-innocent prodding

pump your veins full of moonlight
let your beast drink me in with the stars

remember,
lungs find the inhale and exhale difficult
when there are punctures left in their lining

try to leave mine intact
when you go
don't steal my breaths
even if I make it easy

I have a foreboding instinct
staples and glue
won't be enough to repair me
when you exit

my, how the tables have turned

Unleashed

tormenting,
you lead me
to wander the fringe
only to the deny me

fluttering luscious lashes
test lacy, burgundy bindings
perusing for a glimpse
of your hidden, heated irises

I claimed I wouldn't beg,
yet I find myself pleading
for the ardent demand of
your sinful lips to graze,
to tease and taste,
to brand me yours

my crystalline core
designed to shatter
at our foretold melding

reconstruct me from
within my inner lining
passion's architect,
intone our fluid design
in spoken argot ripples

untie me
that I might
ravage you in turn
just to rewrite
you on my flesh

silk restraints removed
my panther slinks
from hidden shadows
blood-hued blindfold
lays discarded beside
torn leather wrist wraps

wild things don't need toys
when claws tango in tandem

Leave nothing unscathed

I'm a woman of many addictions;
each, its own season.
after dissecting them,
I've come to understand
my obsession with sensory overload.

you're an undisturbed spring pond,
calling my toes to break its purity.
watching my ripples, I ponder
the depth of their reaches.

you're evening strolls in late August,
when outspread arms search out dying seed pods,
liberating them from brittle, grass-stalk homes.

my fingers stretch, pulling top to tail,
undressing dried-out granules to my grasp.
I hold my filled palm to the sky and watch,
entranced with the way they sift through slits
in my opened fist;
the wind carrying them to distant fields.

you're fresh snow, the morning
after a Michigan blizzard;
I can't help bending to
scoop up a handful of sticky flakes,
ball them up

and chuck them at something
anything really.

it appears I'm destructive to nature's brush.

I find myself in the season of your domain,
not a piece of you I want to leave untouched,
leaving my taint on your fiber,
infecting you with my disease.

you're a masterpiece I have the
compulsion to dip my hands into;
dirty my fingers in artistry and paint my body
with your colors.

you're that delicatessen bowl of
cream cheese frosting,
begging to be swirled on a fingertip,
eagerly waiting to land on my tongue.

I forgot to tell you I was red velvet.
baked to perfection,
I await your delicate designs.

finally, a pastry worthy
of addiction.

take a bite,
destroy me.

Dysania

rotary clock hands melt
midnights between us,
the lonely hour
beckoning dreamers to stir

I pull at you
to span the purlieu between us
knowing your skin will rise to my call
I draw on your mirage
to ride the slivers of silver and turquoise
that streak the weave of our exhales

tangibilities blur into silken threads
where my pinned wrists
quiver beneath your steel grasp

opia's hold breaks
as my eyes lull, uninhibited
finding stardust's glow
behind closed shutters
inside the fitful sleep of
pleasure's unrest

clenched fists soften to
cradle a flushed curve that
the sheets have abandoned

sighing,
I reach instinctively for you
but you've receded
back into the haze of
tangerine mists and the
cool, violet waters of Nod

to tease me again
until the night tide
falls on our shared shadows

Untempered

when heated hearth warms eyes with mirth
I'll ante-up a thrill
and ease you back on bearskin berth
to tempt and tease my fill

a slick wet cube of ice acquired
to trace along your trail
and my besotted mouth inspired
to seek its holy-grail

sweet sweat abides until I ride
I'll taste you on my lips
with melted ice to drip and slide
accentuating nips

when pleading groans from your tongue fall
and waiting knows its peak
I'll heed your hot delirious call
and leave your body weak

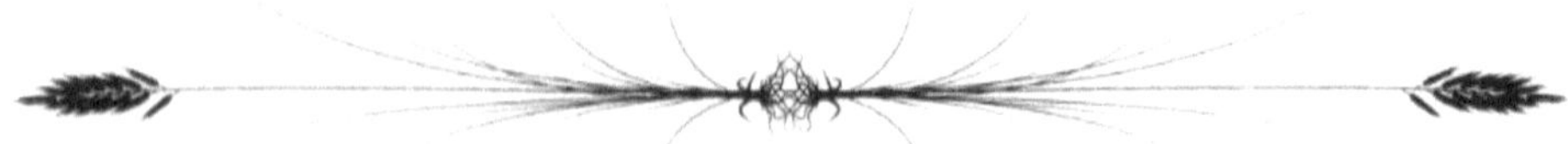

Of electrified afternoons and toes that
tingle

i.
after an epoch of merely existing
you sought me out
as the shadowed shape
that danced through Aengus's dreams

ii.
your calescent touch at my nape
melts away tightly stitched seams
giving you access
to the vulnerability I wear
beneath a sheer opal stratum

iii.
withdraw with me
from the reach of gazes that wander

pull me astride you
where delicate crimson clovers
play pillow to my forearms

run your hands roughshod
through the aerial planes
of our voltaic flesh
as we crash together

iv.
you are precision
in the art of euphoric agony,
a deity I wake to worship

gift me a midday July moon,
on the backs of juniper blooms
while my cursed wings lie dormant
and I, in my veneration
fold into you

v.
awash within exquisite velvet torture
pull taught my every cell
commanding release,
demand on your tongue and
a tug from your teeth on my chest

gliding, we crest infinity's reach
until the quivering subsides

ataraxia sets the stars
receding from my toes
to once again find home
beneath your ribs

The Inevitability of Us

Lured down from my skyward perch,
gold cloak about my thighs.
This man entices shadowed pleas,
demanding greedy sighs.

For eons mortals worshiped me,
the Goddess of the Dawn.
But now he bends me to his need,
the bindings tautly drawn.

Here draped across a shrouded bed,
with bated breath I wait.
As calloused hands do rove and dip,
I'm dinner, not the bait.

A primal urge to claim what's his,
one taste and he's undone.
Velvet ties stretch as I now writhe
and we have just begun.

His fiendish tongue devours me,
no mercy to be shown.
In pleasure's grip, I loose his name,
a throaty carnal moan.

He once was called the Winter King,
for frost was all he knew.
Now fervid shutters melt through ice,
and sinews flare anew.

Cresting waves on weakened sighs,
I'm flipped so I'm astride.
This feral beast pressed flush to me,
is taunting me to ride.

Playful brushes tease far past gone,
spine arched, we rock and quake.
The creature I keep buried deep,
with ceding thrall, I wake.

Gripping tight, restraints are shredded,
these claws seek flesh to score.
With frenzied heat we spark and burn,
to crash forevermore.

Our silhouette strikes memory,
of long ago embrace.
Each iteration found us here,
with fingers interlaced.

Honeysuckle

ceaseless love

The free fall

infinite inhales spent weightless
existing in fragments of a shattered star
plucked from my celestial seat
I am culled through dark wilderness

as a bolide,
I transcribe myself
across vacantly waiting ozone
as a trillion detonating fireballs
burning specters of luminescence
fighting for placement in the heavens

meteorites coalesce into
corpulent scintillating snowflakes
gently descending from a
cloudless stratosphere
their trajectory predetermined

moon glades cavort on
gossamer sheet ice
dissembled guards to the
eminent lake's vulnerable crust

frozen crystals navigate
nocturnal winds
flitting ever nearer the
source of instinctual pull

the finite graze of
flake greeting surface
a cataclysmic shattering
echoing shards melt
in warm submersion
eagerly submissive
to salient alabaster rain

currents penetrate ancient depths
a swirling vortex calls
scattered molecules home
reassembled, my figure glides deeper
breast strokes slicing a path through
inky heat, infusing color into pale skin

south transmutes to north as
murky freshwater streams are
inoculated with sibylline hues
water particles glow in waiting

your hand breaks the surface
to find my reaching fingers
caught in a pulverizing grasp
I am pulled from the water to
behold the world in your gaze
oxygen inundates my being
lungs finally knowing
what it feels like
to breathe

Embracing suspension

heavy lids flutter open
instinct drawing at warm feet
I depart the safety of woven firs
to greet a feeling unknown, but familiar
absorbing the astral sensation
pin pricks navigate the scape of my flesh

your eerie howl reaches eager ears
vibrations transcribing an artery
through the echoes of falling snow

we met for aeonian moments
on Nod's grainy violet shores
yet too often, lost to recognition
finally sleek, sable movements
stalk toward my waking form

hour hands lay as shattered reflectors
crushed under the weight of our waiting
unbeknownst to Chrono's
we traverse brutal brumal tundra
walking the interim in patient hedonism

consumed in memorizing ebony membranes
I wander the inner walls of your cognition
lost in the places our vines intersect

our fertile forms match stride
splitting crisp heimal air
as it strains to penetrate
thermal carnal coverings
amidst February's tenuous gales

we revel in the epoch of our grasp
biding breaths in this season
knowing these storms
we weather in waiting
foretell a harvest unrivaled

take to the ground
my stygian beast
coursing the tides at my side
laze with me
beneath bursting zenith dams
entwining limbs inside starlight rain

chase the dawn beside me

Integrated Gravity

where was I, when first
your claret sang to me
veins straining at the pull
blood reaching multifold
to heed your arduous call

was I spreading seed pods
in the abyssal Grand Canyon
waiting for buds mid-winter
searching empty vessels
for the depths of your eyes
listening to your song drift
the waves of silence trees carry
always there, just behind reach

never quite able to register you
until you rooted beneath my flesh
and all I could do was love you
not a conscious decision,
but an unquestionable existence
your essence fore fused to my DNA
part of me I was incapable of separating

I fell into you
binary meteorites
caught in opposing orbits
careening toward each other

crash coarse set
preparing for impact
impossible

dual universes determined to align
colliding in an explosion of brilliance
alien hues and irregular shapes
the oculus cannot place nor name
the melding of ambits, always known

you aren't simply my now
existing as a singularity
more than my tomorrow
you are my amaranthine

my gu bràth

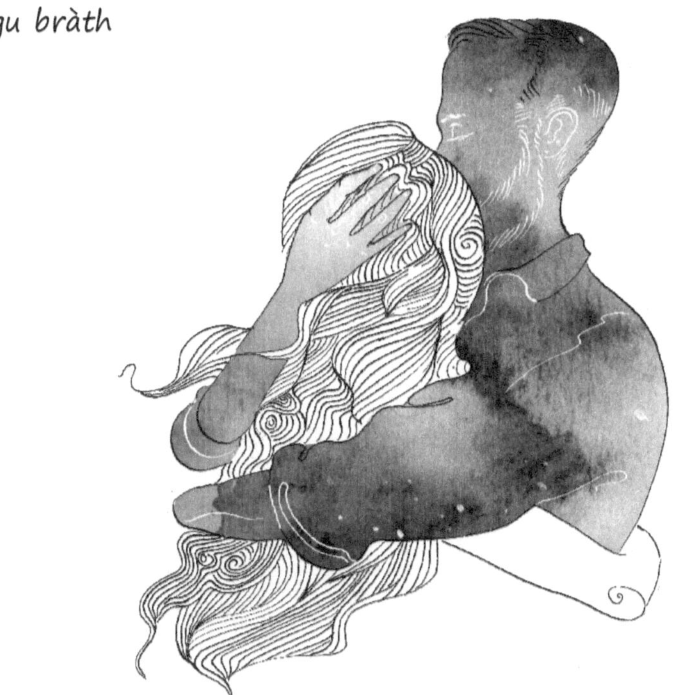

The architecture of us

I count the nights,
the hours sometimes,
in the quiet darkness of waiting

go to work,
dress myself in wanna-be espresso
which falls flat until I smile

these unknown faces
don't surmise my incompletion,
nor guess
that when your sight rests on
the lines marring my sleep-deprived visage
It's you, who grieves
my silent sorrow

this body is merely gossamer
drawn taut across freeze dried bones
until I register the timbres of your voice

you are the portion of myself
I nearly lost faith in
bathing in a silky eclipse that
spanned years devoid of your caress

let free the threadbare cloths
that wreath our separate bindings,
and stitch tightly
the intricate design of us

where once were two
let now be one

Visceral

in lieu of timeworn cobblestones
live coals lined bygone paths
whipping gales urged my flight
flames licking at fleeing feet

ever in search of elusive peace
the spark of memory's embers
drove a restless creature to vanish

    after the fires abated
    I rose from cooling rubble
    to survey the damage
    my fears had wrought

    dawning awareness
    settled a tentative smirk
    on bruised and swollen lips

no desolation is indelible
and so
reconstruction began

    in moments of weakness
    I retreat deep within myself
    old insecurities rising
    to the surface to fester

inky fingers clawing at my neck
rendering breath impossible
seawater leaking uselessly
from the corners of heavy lashes

you call me out
demanding I face the
demons that haunt me

only to obliterate them
without hesitation or fear

a savage reminder
of who you are to me

you are the archaic byway
I have always been on

an intrinsic destination
seeded in my bones

the innate need to submit to
your fierce and feral command
dominates my once solitary will

lost in the expanse of your clutch
we die a thousand atomic deaths

to live

Exodus

I have the wicked urge to
seize habitual frisson in you

efface 400 miles of blacktop
and fall into the ease of your call

my charge of obligations
morphs now to vestiges of ink

in this rebel memorandum
my declaration of exodus

I name you as my artist, that you might
help sculpt the creature I'm becoming

in this silence hums quaking quietude
ensconcing me in a multifaceted
blanket of vibrating numbness

dangerous predawn wind-chill
threatens morning glitter ice
striking fear into this
ancient decaying skeleton

my ribcage grows threadbare,
worn to ossein under the
erosion of an hourglass' shifting sand

head cocked to the side
chilly reverberations
crest the sliding curves
of exposed cheekbones,
unaware of fissures
slicing through the marrow below

carrying just the slightest
tinge of warmth,
a fledgling Sol
attempts to outfit me in
luteous costume jewelry

with the patience of the dead
I absorb these alternating sensations
before denying the heat
to delve into a frozen tundra

in the absence of your touch
even the sunrise rests perverse
on this hollow shell

and so I stand,
a slave to broken frigid dawns

waiting,
for your chisel to tend to me
mending torn joints and severed cartilage

for blood to become a freshet
through the vacant riverbeds
I once called veins

ardently awaiting,
the windfall of you

Awake inside the gloaming

I should be dreaming
with eyes closed to find you

not pacing
in the shadow
of your departure

I'll wait here,
transfixed by patterns
in the asphalt

evidence of my torment
leaves heavy trails of dew,
salt rivulets that stain
my melting crust

I'd smile for you
but the lie would sink
like spilt oil
where only water lies

falling on chrysochlorous irises
that well know
dreams can't hold me

these lids feel the tug
of midnight darkness,
hands pleading for you to
place your claim on me
to find me

ignite the gold and silver alloy
that feeds our inferno
until it teems with your breath

a glowing beacon
to guide me home

Transpose

September's Aurelian scepter
anoints a northern sunrise
spilling a generous portion
of warmed cream to
ooze through night's sieve

I watch mesmerized
to the ghost of summer

as it sifts through flocculent
ozone ripples, to dust
the first of the emerald casualties

newly emerged blood orange
pays homage

she stretches twisted roots
her talons grasping at
fragments of yesterday

deluded into a dream
where rainbow leaves
never fall

and a harvest moon
refuses to don
winter's bridal veil

the tree adorned
with a thousand colors
will surrender to the demands laid
in Autumn's inauguration speech

ceding to the migration
of the jians
to ignite a November skyline

Bleary and back

current crackles 'cross
grappling eyelids
that refuse to open

akin to the scent of lightning
skimming clear night skies
iridescent and intangible

here I am
lying in our dark bedroom
atrium's song
slipping between inhales and exhales
to vibrate the sheets beneath my knees

but the ceiling is composed of pitch and
the stars are faint and fading

vision blurs to blotches
muted mosaics of cascading pastels
bleeding down a rock face to
pool across the glassy surface

reflections I gaze into
lost to this plane for the moment

you catch the fringes of a twine
I braided too tightly

they unraveled in a measly attempt
at retreating to the places
shadows don't venture

what is it your irises see
that keeps you at my side

I am frayed rope
that comes up short most days but
here you are
hand steady
ever ready to weave these threads
into shapes I remember

your vibrato breaking the haze to
sharpen lines and
call colors back into focus
to once again paint stars
where darkness once encroached

Anxiety's a cruel mistress

beneath the cypress
you'll find me
crumpled on sodden ground
the saturated victim of
an early flurry

will you settle beside me
to shelter us
while I shake from cold

pull me back
when I'm lost to fear

and if my mind forsakes us
remind me

    who we are

Wake Me Not

akin to siren song
the pale's call
draws our flares passed
opalescent blockades
testing obfuscous dimensions

I breathe in your exhale
weaving limbs like letters
excruciatingly tender
in the refrain

fingertips tease
water's unbroken surface
slicing like butter
we are consumed in latihan

eons before
first breath was granted
I went for a dip
in the river of you
many times I drowned
to feel your embrace
yet again I jump
your skin to taste

Mnemonic Pigments

Autumn assaults me with ravaging hunger
on this early morning drive,
a heavy heaping of warmth
blending with the crisp bite of November air

obscurity blankets the atmosphere
fresh rays sifting in to caress the treetops
in shades of gold and saffron
buttery light drowsily coats ripples
lapping at a flame drenched shoreline

riding the inside of a tree-lined wind tunnel,
charcoal brushstrokes lend depth
to waking obsidian dreams
the canopy's umbra playing peek-a-boo
with tousled primrose splotches

lanky wandering mist dampens
patches of blacktop
birthing a muffled strain of white noise
as my tires glide along the road

my lungs freeze when an updraft
disturbs a menagerie of discarded foliage,
cinnabar and chartreuse waltz
backlit by early morning sunshine
beneath a haunted blue-gray sky

I inhale,
the giddy-lightheadedness,
reminiscent of our first call

shivering in my old Sierra
I sat in the parking lot after work
held a cracked screen to my ear
and waited to hear your voice
the hummingbird in my chest
edging to take flight

aware that my existence was irrevocably changed
at your hello
it was a familiar sense of home
grounding me
something missing that
even my butterflies recognized in you
an ease of self

It was hours past dusk four days later
on the inside of that dilapidated red barn
when you confessed those three words

leaning against the cold concreate wall
I just stood there in silence for minutes
eyes leaking at the corners
my lips refused to stop smiling
not even to say it back
but that was okay

already,
I'd silently pledged my days to you
and though it hadn't been spoken aloud or
written in quiet messages
we both knew

the inertia of our falling,
a frenzied kaleidoscope of raw artistry
much like this aerial current of hues before me

I am desperate to take it all in
but the longer I watch,
the more intricate it becomes
and I am enamored
with the undefinable shape of it

exhaling,
I return from my reverie
beneath seasoned quaking aspen
my gaze drifting to verdant vines
creeping along an aged sassafras trunk
to seek out the plump limbs of its neighbor

contrasting the knots of rough bark,
mustard stained leaves
cavort with rebellious dust motes
flitting to rest in the sharp lines of
silver slivers and warm memories

Weekdays without your wild

the first recognition of waking
before I stretch my lids
to dare a glance toward the lit window

that is when your absence
hits me hardest

gazing out frosted panes,
I see you in the early morning rays
filtering through lingering fog
night left behind

something dangerous
yet enticing
I've come to understand this as
a beautifully stark brutality unique to you
    our protector
savagely standing guard that
we might never know hurt

your tenderness is
reflected in the light
grazing blood-orange leaves
as they cascade
to the frozen ground
from undressed oaks

you are the changing seasons,
the midnight sun,
breakers far off in the water
where pink tips the edges
and I can't help but smile
when my eyes are drawn to them

you are dispersing cloud-cover
that leaves a prism in the wake
of icy destruction and

    every
            piece
                    of
            you

    is mine

When there is beauty in being powerless

I'm reminded today
of messages exchanged years ago
when we spoke of that
sad saying

    "whoever loves least
     holds the power"

we pondered the idea
of two people existing, who
loved with every particle
of their being
reaching out to match
the ache of the other

where there was no
most or least
just something
so uniquely rare and brilliant
that any who looked upon them
would recognize it

and what a powerful
thing that could be

that was before
we loved *like that*

back when friendship was
the label we owned
and our own great love
was not yet known to us

as we talked
I let my mind wander
allowing myself to imagine
what it might be like
to love you

we look back
and can't place exactly
where it happened

the falling

it was in small moments
like this
when conversation
seeped between the cracks
in my ribcage
and snuggled up to
make its home
in my chest cavity

Glossary

where you can find some of the more
obscure words and references

Aengus: the ancient Celtic god of love. He first spotted his mate in a dream and knew she was his destiny... after searching hundreds of years, he found her trapped as a swan, he freed her and the two escaped and married.

aeonian: ceaseless, eternal, everlasting

amaranthine: unfading and everlasting

aphonic: mouthed but not spoken; noiseless; silent.

archetypes: copies

aria- an elaborate melody sung solo with accompaniment, as in an opera or oratorio.

ataraxia: a state of tranquility or serene calmness

aurelian: golden

birth-lines: fingerprints

bolide: a large, brilliant meteor, especially one that explodes; a fireball

calescent: increasingly warmer

cerulean: bluish-purple

corpulent: fat, plump or rotund

chrysochlorous: the color of a burnished golden green

dossier: a large file (in this case, many memories of the clear night sky from when I lived far out in the country) **bolide**- a large, brilliant meteor, especially one that explodes; fireball

decamp: to depart suddenly

dysania: a state of finding it hard to get out of bed in the morning.

efface: erase or destroy

epoch: a distinguished or specific point in time, often marking the beginning of something significant

Faoilleach: an archaic Scottish Gaelic term for the first month of the new year. The people of old saw great storms at the end of the time of Faoilleach as prophetic of a bountiful harvest in the seasons to come. The season also known as the month of the wolf

Filament: very thin string

firmament: the heavens (also known as the waters above)
flocculent: fluffy, of a wooly nature
freshet: the sudden rising of a river from a flood; a freshwater stream that flows to the sea
frisson: a sudden, sensation of excitement; a shudder of emotion (tingles on the skin) French origin
glitter ice: the fragile sheet of ice formed from a light freezing rain
gossamer: thin/gauzy
gu bràth: Scottish Gaelic meaning "having no beginning and without end"
hedonism: finding great pleasure in
heimal: cold, pertaining to winter
heliotrope: a light tint of purple; reddish lavender
jian: a bird in Chinese mythology said to have one eye and one wing. Destined to remain incomplete until they find their mate... leaning on each other in order to fly. Their mutual dependence is eternal, lasting through death and rebirth.
Kronos: Greek god of time
moon glade: the reflection of moonlight on a body of water
lambent: softly bright or radiant
latihan: a meditation technique, where you embrace existing and moving as pure instinct, free of thought.
lattice: a wooden or metal trellis style of meshwork
luteous: bright yellow; golden
Miyazaki: a Japanese master animator/director/writer, famous for his beautifully artist storytelling
murk: a haze or obscuring mist
Nod: the world of dreams
nyctalopia: night blindness
obfuscous: archaic word for darkness or devoid of light
opal: a gemstone that varies a wide range of colors, it stands for love, passion, desire and loyalty.
opalescent: brightly shining as an opal (a full prism of color)
opia: the ambiguous intensity from staring someone in the eye
ossature: bones that make up a skeleton
ossein: the collagen of bone, remaining after the mineral matter has been removed.
pale: limits or boundaries to anything, either physical or emotional
piceous: black as pitch

purlieu: a person's haunt or the confines of their range; the edge of a forest

sable- black or very dark

sacrament- an oath or ritual

scintillating- dazzling, emits flashes of light; sparkle.

seraphic-pure or heavenly

sibylline- prophetic and mysterious

sirenic(ly)- bewitching

Sol- name of the Roman god, the sun

stratum: thin layer or coat of a substance

thunderstone: archaic word for lightning bolt or flash of light

transparency: when pertaining to the night sky, the visibility of the stars

transpose: cause to change places -to transport-to transform

vellum: outer cover, something written on

velutinous: soft, velvety surface

toska: A dull ache of the soul; a sick pining

veneration: great adoration or respect

voltaic: electric

vagary: a whimsical idea or fanciful dream

windfall: fruitful bounty or jackpot

zenith: point in time, a placement in the heavens directly above you, a culmination in time

zygomatic: cheek bone

About the Author

Melissa resides in a quaint town in southern Michigan with her husband, their two boys, and a spirited Boston terrier. She enjoys exploring many different styles of poetry from conversational, to abstract and everything in between. While keeping to her passion for rich imagery and unique metaphors, she finds the spark of hope inside even the darkest of corners.

Thank you for reading
this collection of poetry,
Please consider
leaving a review on
Goodreads.com

The amazing artists and pages to find their work

Nataletado/Shutterstock.com 5
Xingling yi fang/Shutterstock.com 83, 182
Cotosa/Shutterstock.com 113
Anna Ismagilova/Shutterstock.com cover art, 16, 50, 90, 130, 140, 143, 146, 154, 156,
Ironka/Shutterstock.com 178
Christos Georghiou/Shutterstock.com 7,
K Mary/Shutterstock.com 41
Alisa Pravotorova/Shutterstock.com 147
andrey/Shutterstock.com _I 21
Irina Ikar/Shutterstock.com 25
Illustration Forest/Shutterstock.com 34
alla_line/Shutterstock.com 37, 78, 133, 160, 174
Michael Vigliotti/Shutterstock.com 46
Shekaka/Shutterstock.com 54
Liia Chevnenko/Shutterstock.com 8, 135, 136, 138
Robert Adrian Hillman/Shutterstock.com 161
Gulnara Khadeeva/Shutterstock.com 134
Eroshka/Shutterstock.com 53
Serafima Antipova/Shutterstock.com 62, 97
Jka/Shutterstock.com 166
bejo/Shutterstock.com 184
fran_kie/Shutterstock.com 66, 74
Dmytro Balkhovitin/Shutterstock.com 84
dip/Shutterstock.com 62
Leyasw/Shutterstock.com 10
Rosadu/Shutterstock.com 17
Maren Winter/Shutterstock.com 29
Galyna Gryshchenko/Shutterstock.com 30
nutriaaa/Shutterstock.com 122
Iya Balushkina/Shutterstock.com 52
marukopum/Shutterstock.com 58
Prasong Takham/Shutterstock.com 61
ArtMari/Shutterstock.com 63
Maryna Lahereva/Shutterstock.com 60
12design/Shutterstock.com 68
LUMEZIA.com/Shutterstock.com 70
Valenty/Shutterstock.com 93
Miss Lychee/Shutterstock.com 101
Jula_Lily/Shutterstock.com 102

Nosyrevy/Shutterstock.com 105
Volha Valadzionak/Shutterstock.com 111, 112
Painterstock/Shutterstock.com 117
suns07butterfly/Shutterstock.com 118
Panacea Doll/Shutterstock.com 120
APM STOCK/Shutterstock.com 123, 124
Supergrey/Shutterstock.com 125, 126
t.karnask/Shutterstock.com 128
Holo Art/Shutterstock.com 149, 150
KOSTART/Shutterstock.com 170
Karma3/Shutterstock.com 177
Tanafortuna/Shutterstock.com 180
Eshma/Shutterstock.com 186
Long Summer/Shutterstock.com 187
ArtCreationsDesignPhoto/Shutterstock.com 172
SJitpitak/Shutterstock.com 193
DODOMO/Shutterstock.com 196
Singleline/Shutterstock.com 116
Alisa Pravotorova/Shutterstock 201